TAKING THE TRAIN OF SINGULARITY SOUTH FROM MIDTOWN

TAKING THE TRAIN OF SINGULARITY SOUTH FROM MIDTOWN

John J. Ronan

The Backwaters Press

The Backwaters Press
1124 Pacific St. #8392
Omaha, NE 68108
402-452-4052

The Backwaters Press

Published 2017 by The Backwaters Press.

ISBN: 978-1-935218-425
Library of Congress Control Number: 2016936020

Cover design by Steve Foley. Typesetting by Susan Ramundo.

Printed in the United States of America.

First Edition

This book is printed on acid-free, recycled paper.

For Sandra

CONTENTS

II • THE POTLUCK PEOPLE

TAKING THE TRAIN OF SINGULARITY SOUTH FROM MIDTOWN

I

THE REASON BEING: YES

THE PARLOR

The oldest of the grand houses along Washington

dates from '84 and is one of our *parlors*,

a mansion with wraparound porches and bay windows

built by a fishing magnate, a great man,

himself buried from home, in the former custom.

Many evenings there are crowds of people and cars,

so a stranger would think *party*, again as earlier,

though absent the orchestra and alcohol—or only sometimes

a pint flask pressed in a corner, a cello.

Mornings, the stranger would guess *brunch*, an awards

ceremony for civic virtue held in the restored

structure, the women's hats and silk bows

another throwback. Like the calm, serious conversation,

the white leather guest book, and the garden.

ARROWHEAD

The bifacial point, found in a potato

field in Maine, is still sharp,

a Micmac weapon or crafted heart

knapped from the whole cloth of stone.

Flint's a slap in the face, elegist

relic only as long as you look.

Says: *crow shadow* and *opaque.*

Adds: *I will exist without witness.*

IN THE BASEMENT

On certain isolated, indifferent days

a bright bar of light will strike

clear across the basement.

Like Newgrange or Stonehenge, except

the basement's not aligned with anything.

The light finds something to do.

It probes bundles of books, the white

washing machine, lingers over

Christmas bins, spots the wine

and LPs, a swing set,

half-empty cans of Artisan Apple

and Pewter Blue, the last lapsed

décor idea, stored here in the dark.

Turning around, you notice the dull,

narrow window that allows light

to angle in just right, without warning,

an accident really because of how

the house sits oddly on its plot,

because of the drifting position of cloud,

because of sun, the season, and the trees.

SMALL THINGS, AND SILENCE

Specs, invented in the Dark

Ages, can't eclipse the B. S.

of battles and Big Men.

Buttons get no bio. Garters

start, the slide rule dies—

a coming and going of the well

done, wonderfully unimportant.

And okay, perhaps in your own

life you remember a first TV,

the dungeons of D.O.S., but when

did elastic pants appear? When

did tamper-proof turn puzzle?

In store before you knew it,

the millennium, a web address.

TAKING THE TRAIN OF SINGULARITY
SOUTH FROM MIDTOWN

As the funnel of everyone in Times Square   *42nd Street*

cascades down the station stairs,

pace and urgent purpose damming

briefly at turnstiles before cleaving

into streams for an 8th or 7th Avenue

train, an A Train, the Two,

and while quick, diverged currents, hot

and breathless, pick platforms, stop

to listen for slivering steel drums

in the wait for translation to work or home,

here, at the side of a narrow island

forty feet under ground,

with a wind-rush and rattle that drive

away agile, enterprising mice,

Ett Tag, Bir Tren,

Mmoja Treni, Een Trein,

Premier Train, Jeden Trenovat,

the red One Train halts

and the motley, mustered public steps

forward, hushed and obscure, hips

shifting at doors in slide-by

witness, separate bodies white

and yellow, brown, black and tan,

pocked or whiskery, whiskeyed, wan,

green, gray, big or bone-house,

the meek, mouthy, angry, lost—

a tourist who trails maps and binoculars

jamming last onto the crowded car.

App-trance and defensive doze,

deft conventions of eye and elbow

mind the tribes. A breath brushes

your strapping hand. The platform passes.

Tumbled from the scrum of Penn Station,   *34th Street*

a handsome hardboy's followed by nuns,

louche in blue loafers, who start

with the tame tourist, a fresh mark,

move to a laptop on a clenched lap,

a plugged hummer, a patient cop,

a girl in a green hijab who quits

her Misbaha to nod at the matching habits,

smiling saints panhandling

their parish—a buxom beauty who pulls

open her purse, offering slowly

to a witness of rapt women as she throws

dimes into the can, *clink, clink*:

"The thing of it is, here's the thing,

the reason. The reason being: yes."

Eyes rise to *Viva Las Vegas!,*

Absolut, a scratched *Cadbury* ad:

Amy + Elvis—together at last.

Morning unfolds. A uniformed girl,   *28th Street*

perfumed and stage-painted, twirls

on arrival, greets the hardboy's attitude

with a teasing parade of school plaid,

half-and-half harlot, ingénue

in salsa, sour grape, Tabu.

Opined widely by a man who makes   *23rd Street*

his mute partner blush back,

a blonde by the busty *mater*, opposite

his signing hands and the black habits,

an icon-minded, common commute

flourishing below Fashion Avenue

in GAP and caps, Jets, Giants,

Puma, Nike and tapestry pants,

N.Y.F.D.,

by the sexy matron, Sibyl who speaks

with sly and cryptic, wisecrack sadness:

"A known fact: apart, anonymous,"

During a door delay in which a pigeon,   *18th Street*

engaged in a serious moral mission,

preens onto the car, the pride of Chelsea,

an urban bird who avoids the eyes

of travelers, they in turn avoiding the bird

behind the pickets of print and posture.

The nuns, surrounded by trousers, smile.

The bumpkin, gaze behaving, smiles.

The worldly pigeon, a positive nodder,

fronts the speechless woman who figures

food with a brown bag at her knees,

and witness-wise, dumb as destiny,

fate or whateverhappenshappens,

eats seeds from her open hand.

Lights flicker. The train, in fits,   *14th Street*

limps to the Village, St. Vincent's.

The sage woman, staring intently

at a dark wood of girders and graffiti,

bristles, bosom and big rings:

"The only rebuttal's love. Longing."

The cars start. Peeper skews

to *Viagra, Visit the Brooklyn Zoo,*

listens to chatter blend with brat-

happy prattle—the porn plot

girl who giggles like tickling and sways,

sailor, to the rock and roll of the train,

mix with tin clinks of a can's

conjured coins, the cluck of nuns,

whole rests from the help-meet

whose pigeon pecks at sunflower seeds,

a tightly fused and multi-tracked

Suite for City in Clickety-Clack.

At Christopher, a drunk curses Christ, *Christopher Street*

easy credit, his mother, the Mets,

warns of the end of the world and laughs.

No one gets on, no one off.

The train stops short of Houston, *Houston Street*

stops in the sealed tunnel. Engines

stop, dull lights die

as bodies breathe an undivided sigh.

Lights on. Off. Tense

whispers worm a blind silence,

stage stripped to underlying time,

a long, long loss of light.

When a Zippo's flicked at the far end

of the car, the steely woman sends

down a candle, the candle slow

to return in grudged transfer, glow

soft on the row of stoic handlers,

godgift and galoot, gangbanger,

faces awake in dim, driven

epiphany, grace held and given.

The hardboy's forehead flames with lipstick.

The blowzy bird runs from a kick.

Lights. Jerk of cars. Lurch.

Shoes shuffle, buttocks touch,

breasts and elbows, *corps de ballet*

in brave, awkward, standing balance.

During the stop's shift and witness,   *Canal Street*

the schoolgirl, in gimmick innocence,

leaves with hardboy and his target heart.

"Scratch and match! Tartan. Tats."

The bird, confident that symbol can solve

for self, takes a seat after Canal.

At Franklin, it's good-bye to the bum, who rises   *Franklin Street*

with help from the hardy nuns, good-bye

to the coupled signers who nod and stand,

fire quiet hand-in-hand.

Riders, their rides ending or begun,   *Chambers Street*

are off and on, fungible, one.

You, with your field glasses and guides,

you become everyone too, beside

yourself in witless, wondering joy,

no longer alone, no longer on the way.

Ett Tag, Bir Tren,

Mmoja Treni, Een Trein . . .

One: existing whole in a sphere,

a numen or essence and no more.

The reason? The reason being: yes,

the breath and brush of necessary witness,

superposition of drunk and dove,

an oracle, blue loafers, love

struck in fugitive communion, our close

going on the warm, coincident cars.

TWO MUCH

The whole number trips

into fiction: deuce digit,

sorrows crying the size

of time—a vertigo works,

everyone Van Winkle.

The dizzy dread an end.

For the lesson learned,

they may as well be right:

imagine these sentences

odd as Ovid's, modern

moved until you're grouped

with gatherers, continents

themselves anecdotal,

sailing a slippery sea.

Exegesis saves: dead

reckoning in Years of Our Lord.

Framing faith, the calendar's

hopscotch numbers mount,

liturgy of the Long Count.

MORALITY PLAY WITH A DOG IN IT

The dog's thought is cut to quick dimensions:

the borders of wanting in, wanting out.

It's grand the way his master's given vision:

Sweeping, serious issues of faith and reason,

life lived as widely as mind allows.

The dog's thought is cut to quick dimensions:

Public rut and road-kill rations,

a lazy pace neither enterprising nor proud.

It's grand the way his master's given vision:

Propriety and time, fine dining, salvation

in the gifts of human heritage, our hand-me-downs.

The dog's thought is cut to quick dimensions:

The pen of the present's invisible fence, rejection

of fate and future in a bored bow-wow.

It's grand the way his master's given vision:

Essence? Eternity? Riddles within and without,

mind gnawing on the big bone doubt.

The dog's thought is cut to quick dimensions.

It's grand the way his master's given vision.

DIVES: A FLY IS ALWAYS IN THE WILD

*There was a certain rich man who was clothed
in purple and fine linen . . .*
—Luke 16:19

With speed a fly escapes the doom

of being birdfeed, or trapped by phantom

glass—windows an amber embalm.

Its colors are metallic blue and green,

a little peacock who continually preens—

consequence chronic in all our genes.

A fly, of course, is unaware of flight,

birds or beauty, *virtu*, appetite—

survival of the fittest, not the bright.

Neither can a fly conceive *transgress*,

disturbing another's stately rest—

the higher power *nettled, vexed.*

Use newsprint with a flick

of the wrist—a light tick

restricts the smudge. Be quick.

AT THE PANAMA CANAL

In the restaurant, the tourists all speak

at once: Japanese, Arabic, Italian . . . ,

babbling and making beelines for the buffet,

kept alert on coffee and dessert.

The room's cool, removed from the canal's

original building, a bleached white

colonial ghost baking in the heat.

It's too tropical for us to watch

under direct sun the resourceful water

lift and lower ships arrived

from Riga, Hamburg, Capetown, Callao . . .

as now, *La Vie en Rose*, Marseille.

Gates close on her stern and she descends,

odd movement directly down,

pushing all our separate travelers'

tongues to the limit of idiom, "Ahhh!"

Dockside locomotives pull *La Vie*

forward and the ship descends again,

the second time to sea level.

Twin propellers churn the dull

water, gates open, and she leaves.

PARIS

Sandy stands to the side of the Sisley, whispers,

"Stillness, so soft, the shadows," respectful of art,

absorbing the Louvre's ancient and sacred mood,

the susurrous reverence that surrounds a museum or church—

worship itself a whisper, "Sweet Jesus."

As later, in the bistro on Rue Saint-Jacques.

Finishing a *tarte de pomme*, she ripples the white,

inspiring wine with secret, fricative whisper:

"Lovers, over your shoulder. Honestly. Us.

Kissing, oblivious. Those decades ago."

Alone in our walk-up *auberge*, whispers

continue, thin and finely divided incense

that ends with someone's "Hush," prince of whispers,

a quiet expiring at gibbous lips, the message

breath, a barely dared, private surprise.

PLACE MAUBERT

Kronenbourgs and cigarette packs litter the grass,

clog the fountain in this sad patch of a *place*,

last stop in a tourist struggle to plumb

Paris: the Louvre, Eiffel Tower, tombs,

finally wine ordered in awkward French

and plopping opposite the café on a filthy bench—

narrowly causing my ass to be absent from smeared

continental pigeon shit and Alsatian beer.

An advertising column revolves *La Boheme, Lancome.*

A couple ascends from the Metro, arm-in-arm.

In the April evening, the anxious rush hour

begins to look more *laissez-faire,*

and when Kelly and Caron assume a Doisneau pose

I snap a quick, discrete photo, choose

by chance the romantic backdrop of *Rue Sauton*

leading down to *Notre Dame* and the Seine.

The fountain's lively. Basin lights crystal

the clear water as it rainbows over and falls.

When the young lovers stroll to the bad end

of the bench my French becomes fluent, fond:

"Discovery of the butt! Lest you affix yourselves!"

They smile naively, fix themselves, and kiss.

BEBOP

Popping meds, I'm ready

for dinner, dentist, sex or exercise,

the last after aspirin and lung spray,

Timing the run to low tide

for firm yet giving sand—a balm

to hips, easy on the knees. To fortify

Will, volume in the living room,

Bach or Blakey, a fanfare for elders,

exiting at mid-movement or a drum

Solo because it lifts the heart to hear

music at the largo start and know

later it continues, reverberant and clear

In the house. While I'm towing bones

slowly through shells and seaweed

on the beach: bebop, effortless allegro.

90 WEST

Casino, Custer, Sioux Empire, World of Reptiles,

Cattle Country—the dog barks at billboard beef.

In hormonal bold: the finger, Fargo!, Gloria + ME—

underpass art, pleistocene for its animist air, *Gloriana.*

The radio, too, sounding it out: curler kits

and hog auctions, hectoring hate from the faithful,

and oddly now in slanting sun, the Met pumping arias

into the car, Bellini's *Norma* also heroically home.

The dog's indifferent to *bel canto* and Custer, the voodoo

of his owner's attitude: now, never, identity, Dakota . . . ,

sees by means of bark and bone a selfsame world

in focus, fixed, like some whipped hick of a kid,

premise passion—the lucky dog's not lost.

Signs for rocks and fossils, beer, slush, Rushmore,

rolling now under Sextant, Hunter, Bear and Bull,

a pitch-driven naming of place. Cars drift

and pass, overlap, leave. At Murdo, Mountain Time.

A PORRIDGE MORNING

I'm shoveling to the car, the snow a foot

deep and heavy, breath like a ghost in the cold

February air, the snow white, white,

and I'm remembering my mother at a parlor window

in the 50s, staring at snow in wonder, my own

attitudes toward snow and wonder just forming.

Soon, she'll spin to the kitchen: cup-compulsive

measuring over erratic gas flame, energetic

boiling on the Magic Chef, the pot top

rattling at last over a slurry of hot

oatmeal, brown sugar, butter and nuts.

At the table, she stabs ash into an empty bowl,

wonders about snow—how cold or white,

the depth, the feet-deep snows of her youth.

She's thirty-four, wrapped in a black bathrobe,

chattering non-stop about snow and cold,

chattering about the night's storm, the danger of drifts,

chattering too as she bundles me beyond movement,

finds a plastic shovel, says intently:

Easy does it. . . . And, *Remember to bend your knees.*

Because the snow's blinding white, I grab

sunglasses from the dash, tackle plow peaks

at the end of the drive. Thinking still of my mother,

I do remember to pace myself, and for whatever

wonder's worth, I bend my knees.

THE PURSE

We're off to the service. I ask for antacids.

Sandy rummages from the back of the wagon

a black, unnerving purse: the florid

Ornament and bronze handles, the fashion.

She clicks open locks, plumbs

the magically deep leather: pens

And print pictures, coupons, a comb,

rolls of stamps, a phone, keys . . .

and two sticks of fuzzy gum.

I mention vanity and show, the pricey

interior of red silk crepe.

"Knockoff," she says, "Hermes."

Adds, "Greek for gussied up,

the plush look on a narrow budget,"

returning perfumes and powder, lip

Gloss, lotions, cream. . . . We shoot

past our designated exit, distracted

by luxury and lining, the Juicy Fruit.

DIVES: AT THE UNITARIAN UNIVERSALIST CHURCH

There was a certain rich man who was clothed
in purple and fine linen . . .
                                    —Luke 16:19

Here's your lucky elect: the sub-sect

protestant, patron of positive thinking,

boycotts, brunch, services absurd

with poetry and applause in a house

of brilliant whitewash and light.

It's different in division one:

appeasing kneelers, *mitzvot* maze,

Ghost or Gehenna, lugubrious Jude,

the Covenant scolding, "No, no, no!"

Jews and Catholics know you can lose.

Give me Godgrudge!

Fear of the Lord!

One-on-one with Original Sin

and hell to pay for heaven's hazard.

Psalms say the calm heart's happy.

Others doubt it.

The soul needs demons, don't!

BREAKFAST AT BLOSSOM STREET

There's hot oatmeal for comfort food,

croissants and fruit at the *faux café*

off the corridor to Cox I,

exposed but close tables, a crowd

of docs and patients, nurses, gurneys:

"Hematocrit, lymphs, nothing to do . . . ,"

"The neutrophil (something) stained blue . . . ,"

"I go 'whatever.' Meant it, too."

We dusted cereal with sugar and nuts,

sipped coffee, feeling snug

out in the open, almost amorous

with the hints of honeymoon, one day

asking, could we bring baguettes? A bottle?

The girl, laughing along, loved

le vin, dug the cuddling, didn't think so.

We'd hold hands across the table

in soft, confiding silence, or whisper

the sweet nothings of labs and stats—

a March, an Easter, an endless spring

of tests, treatment, the occasional Danish.

We smuggled in the split and paper cups

unnoticed—only a savvy wink

and nostrum thumbs up from the counter.

We toasted Paris, toasted Bordeaux,

toasted platelets and porridge, vowed

to be wise with side-effect time—

holistic humor, the cheeky placebo.

We toasted traffic and crowds, commotion,

closed with a shameless civic kiss.

II

THE POTLUCK PEOPLE

THE LESSON

The Newtown kids weren't thinking of Aurora or Tucson,

they had not pledged themselves to weapons, and being kids

couldn't remember Blacksburg, Columbine, Binghamton.

The earnest boys and girls of first grade

weren't linking patriotism to firepower and stripper clips,

nor Christmas to domestic terror, cowardice, Congress—

hadn't learned the rhetoric of re-election and leadership,

nor yet had alphabet enough to fathom madness.

Hands over their hearts, the kid-citizens

called out *justice, allegiance, republic,*

the lofty thoughts of American civic prayer

made a persuading faith by the pitch of children:

simple witness and common sense, the mix

of law and love, indivisible communion on a dare.

WALLPAPER

Aardvark's before Bee and Cat, Donkey

in the sunfast jungle, spelled animals who stop

in white panels of wallpaper, accept

briefly their tame, burdened purpose and recede;

the way a Cheshire cat leaves its teeth,

Aardvark leaves an A. The lesson develops—

wide meaning on a legend-layered map,

unseen, rising finally to the regardless eye.

The creatures themselves continue naive as Genesis;

Lamb knows nothing, Nightingale nothing,

as their images thin and turn, trailing off

into the fog of the white wall, free and fabulous.

In their wake, in the kids' white room, a bewildering

kingdom of names and knowledge, a belled self.

AT THE MUSEUM OF MODERN ART

Photography's third floor, the brochure

announcing pioneer artists and old

prints of the liquid labial school—

albumen silver, gelatin silver.

Turning a corner, you're stopped dead

by Eugene Cuvelier: *Will*, in a bare

wind-tangled tree—who knew

they were saying everything in 1860?

And by Auguste Belloc, whose sitter, unnamed,

presents nevertheless with pride and attitude.

In '99, Gertrude Kasebier

speaks of attitude and self and hope,

as after her White, Modotti, Albers,

and Ilse Bing, if you can believe it, in the '30s.

For perspective, the curators include Cygnus

by the Henry brothers, Paul and Prospere:

star-spatter, light-years wide,

shot to correct our relentless spin,

no sliding lines of time trace

but points of light stock-still—

each like a faint magnesium flash

sparked by someone looking back.

As certainly, in Cygnus, there are other cities,

Sunday afternoons, Modern audiences

individual in dress and piercings and hair,

who with simple syntax gasp, "Ooooh!"

at the early evolution of photography, a process

demanding silver and somewhere else.

THE SILVER COMET

L'ordre? C'est la mere de la haine . . .
—Albert Camus

The Comet model's

a syndrome in itself:

fat fenders and bells,

balloons, a brimming basket.

Between the earflaps,

a flat, immaculate face,

a boy of thirty-three.

No apple for him.

No tree.

Other traffic's bound

for the mall or back

from the mall—*Shit*

Happens, Jesus Saves.

Parents clack in spasm,

children savage as rats.

"Hey, nutty!" they yell,

or "Whoop, whoop, whoop!"

Nutty never looks. Can't

afford to look and keep

the Comet balanced.

Saddle shoes and the holster

tell you that. A calm,

waking face pumps

the wide wheels forward,

raveling asphalt, turning

corners over and over,

a dead bird, Bert

and Ernie, your own

assumptive self

captive in the basket.

THE RIDE OF MY LIFE

The signs say sixty

miles an hour, sixty

degree angles, eight

bucks for two minutes,

and *Don't Stand Up!*

My son and I pay

the eight, climb in the car.

The Big Guy who draws

down the lap bar

tight as a tourniquet,

says: "Stash the glasses,

the pen in your pocket.

Stuff flies out."

Cogs catch. The cars

quake, start awkwardly

forward as my wife waves,

safe on West 10th

and others stroll Surf,

Coney Island tourists

not thinking about the Cyclone,

or the comic fate that leads

in the first place to Luna Park,

no way not to be

in a roller coaster seat

at the top of the first drop and . . .

Ohmygod! Ohmygod! Ohmygod!

Up plummet of guts

plunging down, fist

full of fear in the heart-

sick final mind:

I am not on a metaphor.

I am going to die.

Followed by a slow coast,

an arc of confident calm,

balm of Brooklyn below and . . .

Ohmygod! Ohmygod! Ohmygod!

Death drop and keister

clench! Easy screaming!

. . . and the balm of Brooklyn below.

Ohmygod! Horror . . . and hope.

Ohmygod! Horror . . . and hope.

Slowly, slack in the lickety-split.

Speed evens out

and the sine curve dies,

finally flat in a slow

fan turn to the ramp.

The Big Guy hovers

above the cars, smiling:

"Second ride's five."

GA-GA FOR THE GREAT POET

The papers say he'll stroll with notes

up and down the baking beach.

I'm after an autograph, acolyte

Mad for metaphor, looking to match

a faded book jacket photo—

the posed poet, looking crucial.

No clue if he's social or cranky,

or even what I want to say:

"Hello, pal? A pearl please?"

If anything. Soon, the sea,

a nip of gin suffice,

beached brain a sounding

Shell under blue sky—

Collected Works a handy headrest,

pillow series of important poets.

Who are usually, by the time you find them,

dead or stopped drinking,

said their piece already in the poems.

THE ENTIRE CANON OF WHAT'S HAPPENED SO FAR

A gnat steps in resin, cries at the slow,

tissue-fixing, Jurassic sap, "Oh, crap . . . !"

The hapless man from Tollund wails when he's led

by dour elders into the bog-blessed wood.

Thus, Etruscans offer Leinth a wine

libation while water clocks drip, drip

toward Christ, credit and the NFL,

and Joan, pegged to Rouen as sticks snap

and crackle, prays for something like superposition.

Later, Boleyn conceives as Henry heaves

away his weight, the Queen flat as a fossil.

    (All this brought to you by Omniscient Point of View

    and Deconstruction, which says the least of us is true.)

Here's history: statues, strata, amber, ash—

Grecian urns etched with sacrifice and sex,

a form later evolved to flicks and pixels,

faster graphics—Bogart and Bacall parade

behind a goat, flambeaux, priests to puzzle the guts.

And who knows what we'll do with truth? Refusal? Get

of death bred by mind on the mechanism mud?

With ego? With anger and gnat-span? Elysium?

GOOD HARBOR, HOME

(Anthem for Gloucester)

Waves break on outcrop rock: granite,

fire-formed and hard, headland granite—

no coddled cape, no sandbar,

nothing soft in her city, no knickknack:

Gloucester-by-God, attitude granite.

The beaches are broken by wetland, woods of oak

and pine, grace in paintscape chasms, coves,

the harbor of ships, sailboats, a fishing fleet

today inner-harbored, home from the beast-broth

sea, safely moored to Cape and continent:

Cookie-cut, cradle states of the seaboard,

rust-belt, Bible-belt, rivers

priming the plains, Mississippi, Missouri, Illinois,

the corn of Illinois and Iowa, the Dakotas, Kansas,

squared-away states stretching west

to the Rockies, Cascades, a rival coast and ocean—

our daily wake, the entire entrained nation.

Its originals: Ojibwe, Pequod, Agawam, Pawnee.

Later, tribes of Irish, Latinos, Italians,

Poles and Portuguese, Africans, Asians. . . . We,

the potluck people, power in this rare republic,

experiment America imagined over the land, are aged

or tender, bold or shy, yet rulers by right

and by law, the law of nature and of nature's God,

true believers in clamor and compromise, believers

in reason, and so debating rights, wrongs, damning

terror and terrorists in just, seething sorrow,

yet protecting loudly law, the process of law,

stunned as the young to stagger and strut at once.

The noise of debate makes music. Now

playing in this sacred city hall, home

of mellow music, the oaths of public office,

friends elected in a free, local vote

to swear and serve under one weathervane,

minded by murals on history and honest government,

nothing abstract, far away or federal,

servants and citizens balanced in the same boat,

the ship of state a schooner, grand as Gloucester,

seaworthy, wise in the rhythms of salt water

and safeguarded today in the good harbor, home.

What matters happens here! We,

each of us proud, elect, the people of Gloucester,

by law and by luck neighbors in a great nation,

trust power for a term to others, themselves

strong in our common strength, the cast of democracy

in time and tide, a city's lapstraked lives,

and so blessed, confident of grace and granite, bear

witness to America on the broad, abiding sea.

THE FIVE GOOD-BYES

At the back door, Sandy says, "I'm off."

Hates to go, has to go, is going. . . . One.

Lifts her purse: "I said, 'bye.'" Two's petulant—

I'm reading the sports page, fall's

first football scores, obits for the Bosox.

"Kiss?" Three's a kiss, the walk past our garden

to the dusty drive where she turns, torn:

"Water the roses?" I'll water.

"Call?" I'll call.

Four's a doleful, over-the-shoulder, "Soooo . . . ,"

the saddest in our trailing stages

of separation, at the house or airport, over the phone.

Women like five good-byes. Men, no: "See ya!"

The easy relief of wise-guy distance: "D-Fense!"

Buckled up in the long, black wagon,

She drives off waving five, "Good-bye."

THE CULPRIT TONGUE

A lollipopper.

A jack-in-the-box.

Booer of bums,

licker of chops,

the stamp act.

In corners, forked—

busy constrictor.

In cheeks elliptic.

In love, longer—

frank feather,

pert peninsula.

Honeyed, lashing,

biting, bitten,

cat-got, wagging,

held or given.

A dense digit

tied and twisted.

Shuffler of grub,

busboy escaping

the nick in time.

Alone as the liver,

alone and red

as the heart. Holy

hermit waiting

for wafers, always

reaching, always

reined. Bated

flame of larynx

and lung, culprit

tongue summing

sense in click,

fricative, liquids,

labials, dumbstruck

"Ahhh" at the doc's.

DIVES: PROPOSING

*There was a certain rich man who was clothed
in purple and fine linen..*
—Luke 16:19

Place your fingers

on my hips, my thighs—

I'm only corpus,

skiddish-skinned when wet,

now clothed, now nude.

Naked, I'm merely healthy,

sans titles, land, money.

The body has no pockets,

stomachs are not wealthy.

Yet, I am here, I am felt,

and neither are you pearls, my dear.

I'll place my fingers

on your hips, your thighs—

we'll come to love

each other by and by.

FLAT LINES

First: *It's treatable.*

Then: *We got it.*

The docs are always

Pleased with your progress.

For a subsequent spot,

further *Procedures.*

Again: *Got it.*

Also: *Good news,*

it hasn't moved—

a poultice of words

the best of meds.

Later: *Liver.*

Later: *Lungs.*

Enemas, OM,

desperate prayer—

promised piety

tempting heaven,

hedging hell,

the *Courageous Battle*

that's standard with cancer.

As: *I'm sure he can hear you.*

And: *He'd been doing so well.*

WAKING WITH AN EXPECTATION OF PAIN

At the clinic, the doctor explained the routine exam,

its slight discomfort, her words reassuring and warm.

Actually, I hadn't slept at home, so "waking"

is my own cozy—Humpty Dumpty, master of meaning.

And to tell the truth, pain wasn't the real worry.

It was . . . Oh, what's the word? Mortality,

The topic raised by tests, pass or fail,

the end of sense entirely beyond the pale.

Turned out, the workup never rose to nightmare.

Discomfort, sure, but a bearable despair

survived on tranqs and lidocaine locals,

a grim wince the doctor thought was a smile.

THE DONOR MOW

Mowing on borrowed blood, three units,

hematocrit back thanks to anonymous generosity,

and, decades ago, surviving with an implant

From a homeless person who died without ID,

means that nameless men, or a couple, or two women

as I prefer, no longer lying entirely

In a sinkhole cemetery, the humid loam

of an unmarked plot, or in the other case a flat

chaise, sipping cryptically a rickey or rum,

Have become another in a particular garden, startled

by the smell of timothy, the quickness of wrens, the June

extension of hot afternoon sunlight

That allows a donor mow so far from their own

awareness, one in the grave, the second alert,

myself transcendent, spelled by a Bacardi and bones.

MARY SHELLEY AND THE KNOCKOUT MOUSE

Biology talks awkwardly about the brain:

stria terminalis, subcortex, infralimbic—

nothing like noggin or knock-on-wood.

As astronomy the trodden, telescoped moon:

Clavius, *Concordiae. . . . Sinus Iridium*'s

better, but who reads Bay of Rainbows?

It's the flint rigidity of Latin, that larynx-

lock on language, and the obdurate slog

of science as it designates and details, conjures

the new, the fangled, the fear in *Frankenstein*.

Don't worry, this won't be a Woe-Is-Us-Poem,

a luddite lamenting of modern, the unknown,

like Shelley with her cobbled creature, uneasy.

Metaphor's the monster, making facts

of the matter bend to invention, nonsense—

noggin or marbles, the mind's eye,

Clavius resolved to muse and moonbeam.

As dose cloud and the comical quark

call physics home from the cold,

so the well-meaning Mother Nature

holystones heredity, the *noir* of Darwin,

and Milky Way the ache of space.

For modern fears, for Mary's, the amending

texts are novelty and the soothing lunatic,

the lab hobgoblin a knockout mouse,

bent depending on the light and lens

of alibi art, the noodle, truth.

DARK MATTERS

In a universe of unidentified dark

matter, no wonder you wake,

anxious in the a.m.'s

bleak bedroom,

roof exploded and you exposed

to the careless stars, cold

beyond the ability of blankets.

The ladder's where you left it, the calendar,

scaffold, hope and hammer,

naive routines you'll need

for a quick rise and rebuild,

wife, career, and coffee

pitching in with practiced magic—

and anyway, who argues with darkness?

You raise the rafters, bind

timbers to collar ties

for the (of course) cathedral ceiling,

protecting sheaths in shingle

and felt, the fabricated day

in lath and plaster, paint,

always choosing blue.

DEATH, A DEFINITION

Looks like: the dry face of age.

Tastes and smells of camphor, bleach.

Feels like: fear, the incisive pain

of tissue torn away at biopsy—

Parent or child, a sibling, spouse,

faith's case for comfort and life

struck dumb by dissenting dust

no syntax serves. Sounds like:

VEGETABLES

In June, we joined a farmers' market—

organic, left-leaning vegetables

and whole grain bakery goods

off the truck Tuesday afternoons:

celery and kale, cabbages, sprouts,

beets and chard and dense breads,

potatoes so correct they come with mud.

Our small senior group of Greens

is modishly aware of wellness, alarmed

by bleached wheat, the pork pandemic,

by carbon and *E. coli*, cancer. . . .

As a kid, I'd house two hamburgers,

hiding carrots and corn my mother

would discover under the dog dish—

a shortcut to popsicles and pie

in the dark, indifference-ridden fifties.

Now, the government prints nutrition

lists on dairy and grain and fish,

slaps *Beware* on beef and bacon,

on coffee and cold cuts, on whiskey. . . .

The eco-friendly old embrace

water and wildcraft, the newest taboos,

low-flow and *Best Befores*—

mindfulness that means a trading off

of Tuesday's virtue, fertilizer, food.

PRESENTS, PLEASE

In 2944, my birthday falls

on a Thursday. But that's getting ahead.

June could be gone. Thursdays. Self

naturally wants context to continue:

seven days, a dozen months,

seasons nudging one another

across a drug company calendar.

The party starts officially at 4:00

with Black Forest and ice cream,

assuming flour and cows, appetite.

Early bird arrival's fine.

We'll prepare favors and funny hats,

icing, a thousand candles for the sheet

cake—assuming chocolate, cherries,

assuming wax and matches, light!

NOTES

"THE PARLOR"

This is the first of a number of poems I call civic poetry, a term I began to use while I was Poet Laureate of Gloucester, Massachusetts. By civic poetry, I mean a poetry of place and witness. I mean poems written for the public on community topics. I mean poetry accessible to an attentive, general audience. And since it is often meant to be read in public, I mean poetry that relies on sound and familiar forms: rhyming tricks, assonance, consonance, regular rhythms, refrain and stanza, couplets, the workhorse sonnet, etc.

"IN THE BASEMENT"

Stonehenge needs no explanation. Newgrange, a passage tomb in Ireland dating from 3,200 B.C., is less well known. Older than Stonehenge and the Great Pyramid at Giza, Newgrange is noted for the illumination, via its passage, of the central chamber at winter solstice. It is near Drogheda in the Boyne Valley.

"TAKING THE TRAIN OF SINGULARITY SOUTH FROM MIDTOWN"

The 1 Broadway–Seventh Avenue Local is a rapid transit service of the New York City Subway. It is colored red on station signs, route signs, and the official subway map. The 1 operates as a local service at all times between Van Cortlandt Park–242nd Street in Riverdale, Bronx, and South Ferry in Lower Manhattan. The stop after Chambers Street, Cortlandt Street, was destroyed in the September 11, 2001 attacks.

"PLACE MAUBERT"

Place Maubert is just off Boulevard Saint-Germain in the 5th Arrondissement, on the Left Bank. Next door are the Marché Maubert, one of the oldest open-air markets in the city, and the Maubert-Mutualité Metro stop. The free thinker and sometime poet Étienne Dolet was burned at the stake here in the sixteenth century, allegedly composing Latin couplets on the way to his execution. A statue of Dolet was dedicated here in 1889 but torn down and melted for the German war effort in 1942.

"THE RIDE OF MY LIFE"

The Cyclone, Coney Island's wooden roller coaster, opened in 1927. Now operated by Luna Park, it was declared a New York City Landmark in 1988 and placed on the National Register of Historic Places in 1991. The Goliath at Six Flags Great America in Illinois is a faster wooden roller coaster, reaching 72 miles per hour. The Kingda Ka, a steel roller coaster at Six Flags Great Adventure in New Jersey, reaches almost 130 miles per hour. I found the Cyclone fast enough.

"GOOD HARBOR, HOME"

This poem, written at the invitation of Mayor John Bell, was read as part of the inaugural ceremonies for Mr. Bell and the City Council in Gloucester City Hall on January 1, 2002.

"THE LESSON"

After publication in the *Gloucester Daily Times*, "The Lesson" appeared on a number of websites and Facebook pages supported by such organizations as the Coalition to Stop Gun Violence (CSGV), the Gun Victims Action Council, New Yorkers Against

Gun Violence, the White Plains Presbyterian Church, and others. The sonnet was also quoted in full on a website calling itself "Hypocrisy and Stupidity of Gun Control Advocates." That site introduced the poem by saying, "Just when you think you've seen it all, CSGV starts resorting to friggin' poetry." I have never been more flattered.

"MARY SHELLEY AND THE KNOCKOUT MOUSE"

A knockout mouse is a laboratory mouse in which researchers deactivate, or "knock out," an existing gene by replacing it or disrupting it with an artificial piece of DNA. The loss changes the mouse's appearance, behavior, and other physical traits so that knocking out a gene provides clues about what that gene normally does. Since we share about 97% of our DNA with mice, knockouts have helped scientists understand cancer, heart disease, diabetes, arthritis, aging, Parkinson's disease, and many other problems.

"DARK MATTERS"

Dark matter is a hypothetical material astronomers and cosmologists use to account for effects that appear to be the result of mass where no mass can be seen.

ACKNOWLEDGMENTS

My thanks to the following publications in which poems appeared or are scheduled to appear:

Café Review: "Dark Matters."

California Quarterly: "The Silver Comet."

The Catching Self (chapbook): "Two Much."

Cape Ann Beacon: "Ga-Ga for the Great Poet," "The Ride of My Life."

Confrontation: "At the Museum of Modern Art."

The Curable Corpse (chapbook): "Dives: At the Unitarian Universalist Church," "The Entire Canon of What's Happened so Far," "90 West," "Small Things, and Silence."

Enhance: "Place Maubert."

The Gloucester Daily Times: "The Donor Mow," "Good Harbor, Home," "The Lesson."

Hawaii Pacific Review: "Flat Lines."

Instigatorzine: "Dives: A Fly Is Always in the Wild."

The Light Ekphrastic: "Death, a Definition."

Milk Sugar: "Waking with an Expectation of Pain."

Nimrod: "Presents, Please."

Poet: "Dives: Proposing."

The Portland Review: "Paris," "A Porridge Morning."

The Recorder: "In the Basement," "Taking the Train of Singularity South from Midtown."

Red Owl: "Morality Play with a Dog in It."

San Jose Studies: "The Culprit Tongue" (published as "Saying 'Ahhh'").

Snail Mail Review: "The Five Good-byes."
Southern Humanities Review: "At the Panama Canal," "The Parlor."
Straylight Literary Magazine: "Breakfast at Blossom Street."
Tar River Poetry: "Bebop."
Thrush: "Mary Shelley and the Knockout Mouse."
Valparaiso Poetry Review: "Arrowhead," "Wallpaper."
Wisconsin Review: "Vegetables."
Z-Composition: "The Purse."

CPSIA information can be obtained
at www.ICGtesting.com
Printed in the USA
FSOW04n1622190117
29832FS